Why Run When You Can Drive
and Smoke at the Same Time

Why Run When You Can Drive
and Smoke at the Same Time

A MEMOIR

Patrick Leber

Copyright © 2020 Patrick Leber
Author and Copyright Holder: Patrick Leber

All rights reserved. This book or any portion thereof may not be reproduced or used in any manner whatsoever without the express written permission of the copyright owner except for the use of brief quotations in a book review.

This book is a memoir. It reflects the author's present recollections of experiences over time. Some names and characteristics have been changed to protect the identity and privacy of their families. In every story, the author did his best to tell a truthful account of each situation.

First printing: 2020

ISBN# 978-1-7340450-0-0 (Paperback)
ISBN# 978-1-7340450-1-7 (EBook)

Library of Congress Control Number: 2020900170

Printed in the United States of America

Edited by Andria Flores

Cover and Illustrations by Carly Mitchell

9 8 7 6 5 4 3 2 1

FIRST EDITION

Patkat Publishing, LLC
Mentor, Ohio

Questions and requests for additional copies may be directed to:
Patrick Leber
contact@whyrunwhen.com

www.whyrunwhen.com

Dedicated to those who
run for the health of it

Author's Note

Rock and Alternative music have made a huge impact on my life growing up and living in the suburbs of the Rock and Roll Capital of the World—Cleveland, Ohio. Each story is tied to a meaningful song title which brings back a flood of memories regarding that running story. I hope you enjoy the playlist. The song titles span nearly 50 years. See if you can guess the musical artists before reading the reference page. Cleveland rocks!

This book is a collection of essays, and is not meant to be a chronological account.

Stories

"Given To Fly" [1]	1
"Runnin' Down a Dream" [2]	9
"Rock You Like a Hurricane" [3]	13
"Unthought Known" [4]	17
"Good Vibrations" [5]	21
"Comfortably Numb" [6]	23
"San Francisco (Be Sure to Wear [Some] Flowers in Your Hair)" [7]	27
"Stairway to Heaven" [8]	31
"Feelin' Stronger Every Day" [9]	37
"Ants Marching" [10]	41
"Hair of the Dog" [11]	47
"Another Song about the Rain" [12]	51
"Once Bitten, Twice Shy" [13]	71
"Shapeshifter" [14]	75
"My Body" [15]	79
"Lose Yourself" [16]	83
"Machinehead" [17]	87
"Basket Case" [18]	93
"Float On" [19]	97
"No Time" [20]	101
"Hurt" [21]	105
"Ocean Breathes Salty" [22]	109
"Lucky" [23]	113
"Thank U" [24]	117

Prologue

When I set out to write "Why Run When You Can Drive and Smoke at the Same Time" (more on this title in a bit), I did so with the goal to share some light-hearted tales about my personal running experiences. It's easy for me to share these stories in person as I have done over the years, but I wanted to challenge myself to put them down in writing in hopes that they resonate with both runners and non-runners alike. There are many who have run far more miles than I ever will. There are many who will run for more years than I ever will. There are many who will run faster than I ever will. But I figured out that my true passion was running for the health of it. Therefore, this book is for those, like me, who run for the health of it.

It's hard for me to believe that over the course of 40 years and 17,000 miles, I have only had a few running-related injuries that took me to a doctor's office. Many say they can't run due to their [fill in any body part here]. I have been so fortunate and blessed with the gift of glide that I thought I'd share some interesting running stories for those who may have wanted to run, but could not; for those who feel they don't run fast, but actually fly like the wind; for those who don't like to run, yet may find the inspiration to begin; and for those who simply enjoy smiling at the amusing and embarrassing situations I have found myself in while running.

For example, I recall a summer run when I was attacked by kamikaze flies in Williamsburg, Virginia. I label them as "kamikaze" because they darted directly into my face. They showed no signs of letting up as they continued to pelt me over my three-mile home course. I'm sure the neighborhood was impressed watching me run for exercise while simultaneously practicing my karate moves. There are more stories like these in the pages ahead. After reading these stories, let me know what you think at www.whyrunwhen.com.

The glide I have felt for years is evolving into noisy creaks and pains, but what a run it has been…so far.

Patrick Leber

"Given to Fly"

Running wasn't my first passion. When I was very young, I found myself fascinated with rock music. My earliest memory of being mesmerized by rock and roll goes back to second grade when I was six or seven years old. It all started by listening to songs on the radio; the music resonated with me. This led to listening to 45's, 8-tracks, and albums. I associated song lyrics or song titles with situations going on in my life. Many of us do this as adults, but I can clearly recall how music and lyrics affected me in my early school years and continues to this day.

Growing up in greater Cleveland, Ohio (the Rock and Roll Capital of the World), I was also obsessed with watching rock performances late into the evening on an old black and white TV. I have many memories of staying up late to watch *Don Kirshner's Rock Concert* or *The Midnight Special* in which I would enjoy seeing and hearing some of the bands who would become my favorites. I would also find these performances from the late

60s and early 70s at odd hours of the evening—or maybe it was the morning. I recall forcing myself to stay up late or fall asleep on the couch, only to wake up later to surf the three networks for any music broadcasts. *Yes, only three networks.* These older videos still capture my attention when I come across them.

When I was 12 years old, I was so lucky to land a job at a music record and tape warehouse (Record Shack). We were the middle-man selling to the record stores. (I know I'm dating myself here with a reference to record stores.) My mother worked there, which is how I was fortunate to land a job and get paid under the table in my early years. After school, I would ride my bike about three miles to get to work. I started cleaning the bathrooms but eventually worked my way up. I landed in the shipping department where I would separate all the records, tapes, and accessories into list prices based on the code on the spine of the records or tapes. I was the youngest person in the warehouse, working with many 20- to 30-year-old baby boomers and having a ball. Many of these Record Shack rockers remain my good friends to this day. I thought I had locked down a summer job there for the next three to four years while my adventures took me off to college. But by 1981, the record industry declined tremendously, so I could no longer count on a summer job at the company I was so dedicated to. Six years at my first job, I was only 18 years old.

The summer after my freshman year, I was a gas station attendant in my hometown. Then, in the summer after my sophomore year, I worked a landscaping job in Longview, Texas while staying with my Aunt Kathi, Uncle Paul, and cousin, Kelli. It was there that my landscaping co-workers asked me if I had heard of MTV. I had heard of it, but I had not seen it. Some of my co-workers had just added MTV to their cable system and invited me over. *Booya!* I was glued to the screen just like Carol Anne staring at the TV static in the movie *Poltergeist*.

My obsession and love of music has never faded and is a reflection of my innate ability to stay dedicated to a passion. I am an active member of the Rock and Roll Hall of Fame in Cleveland and hope to be for the rest of my life. As I reflect on the word *dedicated*, I think about how I worked at one place from junior high through high school. I have been dedicated to my wonderful wife, Kathy, since tenth grade. Kathy and I dated all through high school and college leading to our wedding after college graduation. And then, there is my dedication to running.

Running gives me the same sensation as music. Call it a rush. They both give me a sense of meaning about my life with its ups and downs. I may have had a bad day, but when a song comes on in the car, it can completely change my mood. Songs and lyrics bring up memories that create happiness, which help me forget about the reason I was down. Some of the songs also bring up sadness, as I tie them to a personal memory. But music instantaneously changes my mindset. Running has the same power to alter my mindset very quickly. Music and running help me convert a bad day into a day of reflection on everything I am thankful for.

I was very active growing up. I always wanted to play pick-up games or organized sports. I enjoyed floor hockey, roller skating, dodgeball in gym class, ice hockey on the Lake Erie marsh, swimming, baseball, basketball, and football. I probably played every sport imaginable with a youth organization or created a version of it in the yard to play with my sister Pam, family, or friends. I was also very interested in the numbers behind sports. I would watch many Cleveland Indians, Browns, and Cavaliers games and figure out how to keep score. If I wasn't taught how to correctly keep score, I came up with my own system for keeping statistics.

At the same time that I started working at Record Shack in sixth grade, my school gym teacher, Mr. Rik Danburg, used an 8mm camera to film me scampering across the gym floor. He filmed a few of us for his Master's program at Cleveland State University working on a project called "Movement Analysis." The video he created of me and others from the 6th grade were part of his A+ project, and I am honored to have been a small part of Rik's successful Master's degree. This is my youngest memory of organized exercise/running.

I have thought about those days often and wonder why he selected me for those videos. I recall running on the gym floor to touch the padded wall, spinning around, and immediately running to the opposite wall, only to repeat the cycle. Mr. Danburg was also my baseball coach, so he saw me focusing on that one sport, while simultaneously witnessing me in multiple gym class activities. Over the years, I have been very fortunate to stay in contact with Rik, and I recently asked him why he filmed me in motion.

Forty-five years removed from the situation, Rik was quick with his reply. First, he mentioned my coordination. For example, he shared how he would tie a rope to a tire and swing the tire to teach students how to toss bean bags through a moving object. He told me he was impressed by my beanbag throwing skills. I only wish that years later the swinging tire exercise had a positive effect on my corn hole game.

Another reason he said I was selected for filming was that I took an interest in him as an individual. He recalled how I would ask him personal questions about his schooling and his family, and that made me unique among all the other 12 year olds. He was new in the teaching field and thought it was considerate that a student nearly half his age would take an interest in someone recently out of college with his undergraduate degree.

Wow! I admit that I don't recall being that inquisitive, but what a powerful answer. That response hit me like a ton of beanbags because I admired him for the exact same reason! My mom had just moved, so I was a new kid in school with few friends. Rik cared about me as a student, and I could feel that. That is how I met one of the most respected all-stars in my life.

In junior high, I ran track for three years. I was a sprinter with little ambition to run any distance longer than I had to. In fact, I don't recall ever running a mile at one time during the many practices. I was also a long jumper and high jumper. As a sprinter, I used my quick twitch muscles, leaving my slow twitch muscles in the cinder tracks. I hear those cinders still exist at my junior high.

Eventually, I stopped growing. While others grew, I came to a halt at a gigantic 5'7" tall (thanks, genetics). I began to be dwarfed by others playing team sports. When I moved up to high school, I made the mistake of convincing myself that I wasn't fast enough or strong enough to compete with my peers, so I never joined the track team. Shame on me, as I almost lost the connection with running for good. But something happened in college...road racing!

In the fall of my freshman year, road racing was gaining momentum. I joined a club at school called the Century Club, in which runners receive a point for every mile they complete. Once a person reached 100 points in the Century Club, they received a t-shirt. That t-shirt was the spark I needed to reignite my passion for running and road racing. My first four-mile race in college was a social event exclusively for the guys in my dorm. Forty of us ran, and I came in 20th place. I was pretty proud of myself to finish right at the 50th percentile. The smallest ember was still burning inside of me, but it had been forgotten for a few years. The Century Club, and the awarded t-shirt, added fuel to the tiny flame, and it has been burning strong ever since. Unfortunately, the prized t-shirt ended up in the rag bin once out of college.

"GIVEN TO FLY"

The Century Club set the stage for me to start tracking my mileage. Forty years later, I am still keeping track of the many miles. Being a stat nerd, this effort would not surprise my family and friends who know me best. Over the years, I've transferred from paper records and logs to electronic records. But, who's counting? Well, I am! I'm not really sure why I find it fun to collect, save, and analyze the numbers, so I simply pass this off as a character flaw and continue to run forward.

Note to self: Remember the past to shape the future.

Year	Miles	Year	Miles
1980	100	2000	571
1981	298	2001	472
1982	270	2002	388
1983	327	2003	446
1984	60	2004	461
1985	317	2005	331
1986	406	2006	458
1987	556	2007	427
1988	771	2008	294
1989	1052	2009	281
1990	1067	2010	173
1991	1126	2011	236
1992	479	2012	249
1993	413	2013	277
1994	382	2014	372
1995	502	2015	372
1996	574	2016	266
1997	602	2017	372
1998	627	2018	378
1999	577	2019	476
		Total	17,806

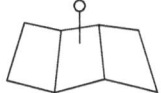

"Runnin' Down a Dream"

Most every runner has goals: maybe a goal to run a marathon, perhaps to run their fastest 5K, or to participate in a triathlon. One goal I've had since I started running is a little unique and more personal to me. I want to run at least one mile in all 50 states. I track my progress with a map at home, highlighting every state I've run in. As I type this in 2019, I am up to 33 states, so I still have a ways to go. Some of those runs were uneventful. Yet, some were memorable. In Nebraska, I ran four loops around an interstate rest stop while helping my son, Jake, move out west. Then there were five loops around the rest stop in Utah while Jake filmed me on his phone. At both rest stops, folks were wondering what I was doing. Nobody had the nerve to ask me, but I could see it in their eyes. *Can't you see I'm running here?* I was able to take credit for running in five states during that single road trip (Iowa, Nebraska, Wyoming, Utah, and Idaho). That trip culminated with a 10K race in Boise, Idaho which produced the coolest race shirt after hundreds of road races in my running career.

I highlighted Mississippi when I had the opportunity to run on the campus of Ole Miss during a business trip. That run came with the need to find a restroom in the middle of the run. Why I even remember that is odd to me. Another time, I got in a great run on the Clemson campus in South Carolina. After that sweaty workout, I felt awkward climbing into my rental car. I could not cool down due to the humidity and felt bad for the next renter. I also ran on the University of Georgia track in Athens, Georgia. That UGA track run was significant, as I hit my 15,000th mile on 7/4/11... Boom, the 4th of July!

I jogged around the outside of the NASCAR track in Bristol, Tennessee. The Bristol run was rather tough, as it is very hilly in that beautiful part of our country. On the way to Tennessee, I ran a few laps around a Wal-Mart parking lot in West Virginia while my dad, Ray, waited in the car for me to finish. I had to seize the moment of being in the Mountain State.

In California, a bird chased me as I ran outside of my hotel. I don't mean one pass-by warning, but he followed me for about 100 yards of sprinting. I guess he thought I had invaded his flying turf. I've had many California runs and enjoyed all of them.

Running in Las Vegas was interesting while people stood out on the corners trying to hand me "Girls! Girls! Girls!" pamphlets. *Can't you see I'm running here?*

Although not a state run, it was interesting to run around the perimeter of our all-inclusive resort in Jamaica. As I approached the front gate, a local citizen on the other side of the minimally restrictive gate asked me if I wanted to buy some pot. *Can't you see I'm running here?* I have also been fortunate to travel the world and run in Canada, Hong Kong, Singapore, Germany, Japan, and The Netherlands.

Thirty-three states down, and 17 to go. How will I ever get to Alaska?

Note to self: Plan future road trips.

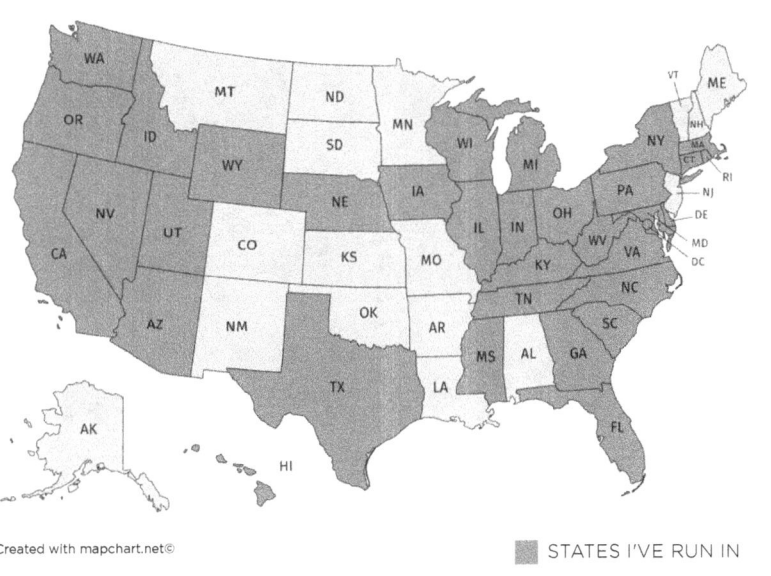

STATES I'VE RUN IN

"Rock You Like a Hurricane"

Our first residence in Virginia was a small apartment near the corner of a busy intersection. My wife Kathy and I were in the process of moving to the East Coast from Fort Wayne, Indiana and landed an apartment in Newport News, Virginia. Kathy had stayed back in Indiana to help sell the house, while I moved to Virginia to begin getting us settled in our new place.

The traffic noise at the intersection of the apartment provided a constant, comforting hum of cars on the pavement. If a car horn wasn't occasionally blaring, there was a siren wailing from the many emergency vehicles that crossed this hustling area. The junction was a three-way "T" with an additional leg being paved to create a new street to make it a four-way intersection. The fourth leg of the junction was not yet open to cars. A 7-Eleven convenience store was at the corner, and our apartment building was right behind the store.

One day after work, I decided to take an early evening run.

The new street was peppered with large steel road signs on their easels reading: "Newly Paved," "Stay Right," and "Proceed with Caution" even though there was no traffic allowed on the road yet. Traffic lines had been painted on the new roadway. It seemed clear that the street was just a day or two away from opening. The large, temporary road signs continued for approximately a mile, and they were at each inbound street that fed into the new thoroughfare.

Before heading out, I heard on the news that a strong storm was heading our way…a Nor'easter. Having lived my entire life in the Buckeye and Hoosier states, I honestly had never heard of a nor'easter. The internet was not popular then, nor were cell phones, so I didn't have quick access to Google to look it up.

I planned to run in the center of the newly paved road. I deduced that while they were allowing the new pavement to cure for the oncoming onslaught of thousands of vehicles, the road was solid enough for a runner to take in a jog, at least according to my untrained construction eye.

As I began, I could see the dark clouds toward the east. At about the one-mile mark, I heard a rumble of thunder. Shortly thereafter, the skies began billowing with menacing gray clouds, and I saw the first streak of lightning. Common sense told me *I had better cut this run short and head back.* So, I listened to the angel in one ear, while the devil in the other was calling me "chicken." Logic said *a two-mile run is better than no run.* The storm was now bearing down so fast that I kicked it into the next gear before the first raindrop could hit me.

I was running back down the soon-to-be-opened road headed straight for my apartment. The wind picked up, then light rain, then heavy winds, then hard rain. It got bad quickly. Lightning was cracking right over me as I watched day turn to night in maybe 60 seconds. I was out in the middle of this brand-new street with absolutely no cover except for tall pines which I had learned to avoid. No other humans were in sight. *Why would they be? There was a nor'easter coming.*

In the homestretch heading for cover, I saw the traffic light at the intersection in front of me with the 7-Eleven across the street. I was now in a full sprint for the store. Still about a quarter mile from the convenience store sanctuary, I had never felt such anticipation to enter a 7-Eleven as I did at that moment.

All of a sudden, the huge steel road signs I previously ran past were whisked off their easels. Powered by high winds, the square signs started rolling, corners digging into the new pavement, as they hurled my way. I was scared to death as all of these heavy metal street signs chased me down! *Was I living a horror film script?* Through the pelting rain, safety was in sight at the 7-Eleven, but the lead actor was about to be cut in half by thin steel street signs coming at him from multiple angles. The signs blew past me as I zigzagged to save my life. I was terribly frightened and having an out-of-body experience at the same time.

I was able to safely and quickly sprint through the intersection since all the traffic had stopped on the road or had pulled into adjacent parking lots to wait out the storm. I was a mental wreck and just a hail stone's throw from the front door of the 7-Eleven. The few cars in the parking lot were only there to avoid the assault of wind, rain, and lightning. I squeezed between two of them to the entry door. I didn't glance to see anyone's reaction to my passing.

I shoved the door open as if I were escaping from jail. Inside the store, there were no customers. The clerk's mouth opened wide and his eyes locked on me as if to say, "…and you came from where?" I was soaking wet as I stood on the welcome mat inside the store. I had just seen my life pass before my eyes when I looked at the clerk and asked, "What's a nor'easter?"

Note to self: Stop being a magnet for wild weather.

"Unthought Known"

It was a warm summer day on my regular 5K loop, which took me on a long, straight, busy street near the beginning of my run in Mentor, Ohio. Runners must use their peripheral vision when crossing driveway aprons, the section where the driveway meets the road. In fact, aprons on busy streets are probably the most dangerous paths for runners. Cars are sometimes turning into parking lots or their own driveways and have not taken notice that a runner is moving parallel with them. All runners need to keep their senses alert when crossing aprons. As I was halfway across a busy apron, I could see a cyclist on the sidewalk opposite me approaching the apron. She appeared to be slowing down due to the pending traffic, the approaching apron, and possibly me coming at her from about 30 feet away. Unfortunately, her front tire caught the groove between the sidewalk and the grass and she wiped out—really wiped out—hard. It took my breath away. Thank goodness she did not go down head first, but her whole body slammed against the concrete.

I sprinted the short distance between us to get to her right away. Witnessing her fall kicked in my adrenaline. She was visibly shaken, crying, embarrassed, and bleeding from shoulder to toe. I moved her bike and helped her to the grass, trying to calm her. Her movement to the grass was precarious, as she could have had some broken bones based on my observation. I wasn't far into my run, so I offered to give her my cotton shirt to wipe away and stop the bleeding. She accepted my shirt and continued to cry for some time. She simply did not want to move.

We were maybe 10 feet away from a very busy street at a bustling intersection with a traffic light, and nobody stopped. I know dozens of drivers witnessed the fall, but everyone drove on. For at least five cycles of traffic light changes, not one person pulled into the shopping center parking lot to check on the woman. Neither those who witnessed her go down, nor the many who were stopped at the traffic light, stopped to check out what was happening. It was obvious she needed help, as she looked like a prize fighter who just went through multiple rounds in the boxing ring. There I was, shirtless in running shorts and shoes, trying to help her up.

Then I noticed that the fallen cyclist was wearing an interesting outfit. She was completely decked out in the color pink. Her hat was a bright pink with buttons, her shoes were pink, as was everything in between. Even her bike was pink! Pink streamers were wrapped around the entire bike frame and wheel

"UNTHOUGHT KNOWN"

spokes, and the same streamers dangled from the handlebars. In the rush of the moment, I didn't immediately take notice of all the pink. Once the situation slowly de-escalated, and I read her shirt, I didn't need to ask why there was so much pink. The fallen cyclist shared that she was a very proud supporter of the Susan G. Koman Breast Cancer Foundation. She was about to participate in an event later that day and wanted to take her bike out to proudly display her support. That leisurely ride took an awful twist in one second.

She tried to stand but could not. I tried to help her stand, but could feel that she needed 90% of my support to stand upright. Therefore, she could not walk. She was really hurting, so we sat back down. *C'mon. Someone, please stop to help.* Maybe 200 cars had passed by when an angel in a white Camry pulled into the store parking lot and asked if we needed help. The driver opened her trunk, where she had clean towels and brought them to the woman. Once our fallen cyclist had cleaned up a little more, we helped her to the Camry, as our angel had offered to drive the cyclist home. Once she was settled and about to leave, I offered to take her bike to her house nearby. After she gave her address, they left to get her home in the car, and I walked back to the bike laying in the grass by the sidewalk.

As I approached the pink bike donned with streamers from handlebars to spokes, it struck me what I was about to ride. So, I proudly sat on her bike, making sure it was in safe condition to ride. Then, this shirtless runner in skimpy running shorts and a wide smile rode her pink bike with decorations flowing from every angle down the sidewalk of the busiest street in Mentor, Ohio on a sunny Saturday afternoon.

Note to self: Always be willing to give the shirt off my back.

"Good Vibrations"

A dog situation occurred one summer between my college sophomore and junior years in Longview, Texas. While working with a landscaping company for the summer, I was staying with my Aunt Kathi and Uncle Paul. Texas runs are tough, as it's hot all the time. There is no good time to run early in the morning or late in the evening because it's stifling hot even then. Still, I was on a morning run through an open field, minding my own business, when I saw a little white dog locking in on me. The dog's bark gave away its discreteness as I caught him out of the corner of my eye. I did not see any human nearby.

"Toto" was a small terrier and appeared to weigh about 15 pounds. While constantly barking, Toto made a beeline for me from about 50 yards away. I quickly deduced that this little guy must have taken a physics class because Toto was not running directly at me, but at a trajectory which would enable him to eventually catch me based on my current path and pace.

I continued with Toto in my periphery, and I thought, *Toto is running a timing pattern just to scare me and will soon back off. Besides, Toto is a small dog. What harm can he really cause?* With no physics experience, yet many miles logged, I estimated that Toto may have miscalculated. *If I speed up, I figure I will miss the strike point.* Although Toto was moving quickly, I believed I could move even faster. But as the trajectory narrowed, I got a little more nervous. By then, I was beyond the point of no return, so I decided to shift gears again and sprint a little faster.

I was only a half-step ahead of Toto's calculation. As the dog flew behind my ankle, I could feel his breath, and I imagined Toto saying, "Oh nooooo! I missed my breakfast."

Toto missed me and proceeded to wipe out, rolling over and over until he popped up and just stared at me. To any onlooker, it had to appear that a missile had just missed its target.

I looked over my shoulder as I continued to sprint forward, and I saw Toto giving me that inquisitive puppy look with a slightly-tilted head. He stood still while gazing and panting with a smile on his beautiful face. His eyes appeared welcoming and happy. I then realized that Toto probably thought this was a game and not target practice. I wasn't going to stop to find out, so I said goodbye to Toto, and I finished my Texas run. Even though Toto had better analytical skills, it felt good to be faster than a 15-pound dog.

Note to self: It's never too late to take a physics class.

"Comfortably Numb"

After my junior year of college, I decided to stay at school in Bowling Green, Ohio and take a semester of summer classes. I did this in order to graduate early while the love of my life was back at home working hard to save money for our wedding. Therefore, it was pretty quiet that summer, and I was quite lonely. College campuses slow down tremendously during the summer, so there were not many social opportunities compared to the fall and spring semesters. This was also long before cell phones existed, so catching up on the phone was infrequent. I found myself running a lot to pass the time.

I had signed up for a 10K race in Toledo, Ohio, which is a short drive from Bowling Green. The primary sponsor was a beer company. I traveled to this race by myself, so I didn't have anyone to hold my gear or to wait for me at the end of the race. It was very hot, and I struggled a bit to get through the race. It was one of those races where, based on the weather conditions, I told myself during the pre-race not to try for a PR (personal record). It's a pretty easy task to predict how I might perform since I have experience running in all kinds of weather conditions. The race itself was pretty uneventful. It was what awaited me at the finish line that got fun.

After the race, I was drained physically and mentally. The running course had very little shade, and I roasted like a marshmallow on the pavement. The direct sun kicked my butt, and I felt extremely dehydrated. There were many refreshing amenities offered beyond the finish line, such as water, sports drinks, and fruit. Though I hadn't noticed during pre-race, this 10K also had beer trucks with taps coming out of the side of their trailers. I thought *that sounds really good right now*. I decided to bypass the water and head right to the friendly servers for some ale after my scorching 10K. The beer was free for runners wearing their race number. *How can I pass this up?*

I drank the first one quickly, as I needed to replenish my fluids. I couldn't have been seated on the curb in the shade for more than one minute before the suds hit my stomach. The first one tasted so good and went down so smooth that I found myself getting another. I sat on the same curb and sipped away on my recovery ale. The second beer also went down just as quickly because I was melting. Still very hot and not yet recovered, I thought *I must really be dehydrated.* So there was no hesitation to grab beer number three.

I picked up the third beer and sat back down on the curb to revitalize my body. I thought it was pretty amazing to be able to drink more than two beers in less than five minutes. *My body must really need these fluids! Have I ever drunk three beers in five minutes? No.*

Bamm!

I stood up after putting away the third beer and started laughing at myself as my leg/eye coordination was way off. I was drunk. I quickly determined that I needed to sit back down on the curb to regain my composure. But there was no composure to be regained, as the alcohol had already settled in. The only chance I had at maintaining some sense of dignity was to make sure nobody saw me laughing at myself.

Whatever I had planned to do after the race was going to have to wait. I needed to get this alcohol out of my system. Since my leg/eye coordination was off, I was embarrassed to try to get up again to fetch water or a sports drink. I was also embarrassed to ask anyone if they would get me a water. So my plan was to sit there and wait for the alcohol to wear off while I stretched and watched the people walk by.

All the runners had finished, the awards were over (thankfully, my name was not called), and there I sat on the curb—still. I was in a good mood. I continued to laugh at myself for falling into the trap of "free beer." I eventually got the courage to stand up and head to the water table for additional fluids long after the third beer beckoned "drink me."

The event was wrapping up, so the water table was being taken down. I was lucky they were willing to pull a water bottle from the stock they were putting away. I sat on the hot curb again for what seemed like forever while the race organizers put away all their race gear. I'm sure they were wondering why I was still hanging around. Bet they thought I was sticking around for the free beer!

Note to self: Never run a race sponsored by a beer company.

"San Francisco (Be Sure to Wear [Some] Flowers in Your Hair)"

One of the more interesting sights I've seen while running occurred during a vacation in San Francisco. Kathy and I had traveled there to celebrate our 20th wedding anniversary while also meeting up with some friends from Sacramento. We all decided to stay at a hotel near Fisherman's Wharf and planned a fun mini-vacation. When we arrived at the hotel, a note was on our bed indicating that the traffic flow may be difficult the next day as the city was holding its annual Bay to Breakers race. *Cha-ching!* Having heard of this race over many years of running, I was naturally excited to learn that it was going to occur the very next day. I had no idea that it was going on that weekend. I recall reading that the crowd was wild and dressed in every imaginable costume. I also read that some are dressed in their birthday suits. The run is a point-to-point event of almost 7.5 miles. Far more people run for the fun of it than for the competition. We went about our normal vacation that day, as I was excited to get up early the next day to witness this famous race. I wasn't going to participate in the Bay to Breakers run. I just wanted to be on the sidelines to watch the many runners and their extravagant costumes.

The next morning, I didn't want to compete with the probable parking congestion, so I put on my running gear and decided to jog to the race. I carried my phone with me to take pictures because I anticipated some interesting sights. It wasn't a short distance to get from our hotel to the race location. That didn't dismay me, so I began running a few miles to the starting area along the Embarcadero. It was a chilly, yet sunny, morning so I truly enjoyed this run while sightseeing along the way. On my jog to the starting area, I came up with another idea. I decided that it would be fun to actually run a mile in the race with the masses. Then, I could peel off from the runners and to head back to the hotel. Once I arrived to the huge crowd already gathered, I sensed that this was unlike any other race I had seen. I saw runners in every possible costume. Many wore costumes I wouldn't have even thought of. I recall a guy dressed as a bag of Miracle-Gro potting soil. There was a group calling itself "Team Jeannie," dressed like Barbara Eden in *I Dream of Jeannie*. There was a tiki bar moving on wheels with active bar patrons. The race had some regular runners, too.

A unique pre-race tradition is to toss tortillas all over the place. This was news to me. Participants were throwing thousands of tortillas like Frisbees all over the sky. I've read that the tradition probably started similar to beach balls at rock concerts. Anyone who gets hit with a tortilla simply picks it up and puts it back in flight. The guy next to me got nailed in the face, but quickly laughed it off. *No harm, no foul.* Having a conversation with one's neighbor increased one's risk of being hit with a tortilla. I couldn't help but think of the wasted food on the ground after many of us trampled them at the start of the race.

There were thousands of runners. The starting group of runners weaved through multiple blocks going many different directions yet funneled to the starting line. The race was scheduled to have approximately 80,000 participants! Everyone was in a great mood.

Once the race started, it took several minutes to get moving. Even once we began sputtering forward, it still took another five minutes to get to the starting line. Once beyond the starting line, everyone was shoulder to shoulder for another few minutes until we could take baby steps. Finally, we could start jogging. After about a mile, I pulled off onto the sidewalk to watch all the runners pass by. Within 30 seconds of being an observer, and no longer a participant, I witnessed my first bare encounter. A group dressed as flamingos decided it was time to take their clothes off in front of me and the other folks on the sidewalk. Gawkers gathered to take pictures as these middle-aged men and women figured it was time to get naked and run. *Crazy!*

I continued to watch the wave of runners pass by while I stood on the sidewalk keeping my eyes open for flying tortillas while taking photos of the amazing costumes. I probably did this for another 15 minutes and then decided it was time to head back to the hotel. I didn't want to leave the event, but I knew we had a busy day planned. I retraced my path backwards on the sidewalk next to the street I had just run. I was amazed at all the unique costumes, and by the number of people who decided to run in the buff. It really was quite entertaining just to watch everyone having fun. I jogged back to the hotel to watch the rest of the event on TV and to share the amazing experience I had just witnessed. Kathy, and our friends, appeared to be slightly disappointed by missing the event. Yet, they were able to relive the party through my pictures. I am thrilled I got to participate in this famous race even if I wasn't in costume.

Note to self: Don't ever run naked in public. It will end up on the internet.

"Stairway to Heaven"

Every once in a while, all people step outside of our comfort zones. After spending countless hours running many miles on the roads, I saw an opportunity to try something different. We were living in Fort Wayne, Indiana at the time, and I registered to race up 20 stories inside a building. On the day of the event, I arrived early, as I didn't fully understand how this was going to flow.

I immediately noticed everyone gathered in an underground parking garage, and I could see the race organizers. As I walked to the center of the garage floor, I saw the stairway where it appeared the event would begin. A race organizer told me each runner had a unique start time. The staggered starts were one minute apart, so all participants needed to be ready promptly at their assigned time. Once I checked in, I was given my slotted time. Now that I understood the race start and had plenty of time before my assigned time, I headed upstairs to see how the finish line would be handled.

I took the elevator with a number of runners who probably had the same question as me. *What does a finish line look like on the 20th floor?* Taking elevators with runners can lead to unique smells. Since it appeared none of us had run up the 20 floors yet, we all survived the ride. The group on the elevator was excited about the event as we chatted heading upward.

Once the elevator door opened, I immediately noticed that everyone was coughing on the 20th floor. This wasn't a typical "I have a slight cough from a cold." Runners were hacking up their lungs. I looked left and right, and the chorus of coughing was coming from every side. I stepped outside the elevator but stayed by the door as it closed. I was hesitant to take one step forward into the swirling winds of the many coughers. I should have held the door and gone right back down, but I was late to react. I couldn't wait for the next elevator to arrive to get me back down to the garage level. *What did I get myself into by signing up for this race?* I did not want to be in an enclosed environment with everyone spreading germs, so I patiently waited for the next elevator to arrive while holding my breath.

I watched one finisher come up the stairway chute and cross the makeshift finish line in the middle of the hallway. Now that I knew how the finish line was organized, all I could think was *get me out of here! What is causing all these deep coughs?* Maybe the air in the stairway chute was very dry causing the runners to choke. It was a cool spring morning, yet the air in the stairway was probably old, wintery, stale air. *Guess I'll find out.* As I rode down in the elevator to the start line, I psychologically prepared myself for what was about to happen in that stairwell.

I had a little time to stretch and warm up before my designated start time. Unfortunately, the underground garage was pretty cold, so I had to keep moving if I wanted to truly warm up. It was finally my turn, so I wandered near the stairway chute to get in line with the others awaiting their takeoff. I mingled with the other runners enquiring if they had ever done something like this. The unanimous response was that we were all stepping out of our comfort zones.

Once signaled, I launched off pretty quickly running up the stairs. Each floor was made up of two flights, so there were to be 40 flights to conquer and 40 wrap-around corners to turn. Around the fourth floor, I began to use the handrail to assist my upward momentum. By the eighth floor, I had to stop running and start walking, which caught me by surprise. I was confident I could scale these stairs with my own body strength, but I realized I needed help with the railing less than halfway to the finish. But I was still moving well by pulling on the railing and scaling two stairs at time. It was also near the tenth floor that I could feel my throat beginning to dry out due to the stale stairwell air. Around the 12th floor, my mouth felt like the Sahara Desert, and I was dealing with a rubbery left arm and shoulder. I hadn't trained to use my left upper body for this event, as it never occurred to me that I may need the railing for momentum support.

I made it to the top with extremely heavy breaths and my heart pounding hard in my chest. I don't recall where I finished in my age group, but I did respectively well. Once I crossed the finish line, the path led me into a side room where organizers had laid out refreshments and snacks. One was a large bowl of carrots.

Being a huge fan of fruits and vegetables, I welcomed the large bowl of carrots in front of me. There was nothing to drink yet, so I grabbed a handful of carrots. I took a bite and immediately the carrot scratched my desert-dry throat, and I started to cough—not just a cough, but a deep, belly-bending, eye-watering cough. I got suckered into the same trap that many others did at the finish line and grabbed what was readily available. After all, carrots are a healthy snack for race finishers.

My coughs were deep and continuous. I quickly deduced that I had fallen into the same pattern as other unsuspecting stair climbers. I had a carrot-cough like everyone else. I scouted out the finish area prior to my climb and assumed the air in the stairway was the cause of my choking colleagues. *My bad.*

I find it easy to laugh at myself, and I thought *here goes another situation.* Internally, my predicament was so funny that I was truly coughing while laughing at myself at the same time. I was laughing so hard that I was tearing up. To the casual observer, I appeared to be choking, gasping for air, and crying at the same time. I finally found some water and decided to go hide in a corner to recover. Many were staring at me, and multiple

"STAIRWAY TO HEAVEN"

people started checking on me. "Are you okay?" they would ask. I gave many thumbs up responses or moved my head up and down, signaling that I was okay, as there was no chance to verbalize my reply. I also found this amusing as I was now worse off than any other victim of the Great Carrot Debacle. One person would check on me, only to be followed by another less than 30 seconds later. I could not regain my composure as I continued to laugh at myself but couldn't explain to anyone why. I lost more body fluid in tears than in sweat from the stair climb race.

Note to self: Never, ever, eat a carrot after running.

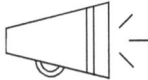

"Feelin' Stronger Every Day"

Although running is part of my DNA, I need motivation at times. Additional motivation came during my first marathon when I least expected it. When I signed up for the marathon, I had a lot of support from my co-workers. After all, they were going to join me and run the marathon, too. They weren't going to run side-by-side with me, as we each had different skills and goals, but we were going to drive together back to my hometown to run a spring marathon. We stayed with my mom and went out to a nice, high-carbohydrate dinner the evening before the race. I welcomed a full plate of spaghetti.

The race day was warm and sunny. Most runners shy away from the heat and humidity, but I love running in it. While many runners struggle in these conditions, I seem to thrive when it's hot and sticky. I feel as if my mechanics improve in these challenging conditions. Still, I'm cautious running in the heat. Mother Nature always wins in the long run. As I have aged,

I find that running in the heat and humidity is progressively more difficult, but I still prefer these warmer conditions in a t-shirt over any cool, long-sleeve jersey run.

One of my first marathon goals was to keep running and not stop. I made up my mind that I would not hit the proverbial "wall," but pace myself so that I could finish the race saying I ran the entire way. I ran very well that first marathon. I was going strong and had not walked yet when I approached the 20-mile mark with only about six miles remaining. I recall being both physically and mentally exhausted. The sun continued to beat down as I was breaking the race into smaller segments in my mind. *There goes another mile. Only a 10K to go. You can do this.* I felt as if I wasn't running anymore. I was plodding. And there, I discovered my surprise motivation.

Without warning, I heard a group of people ahead of me on their blankets and chairs. It was my family! They called out my name as I approached. Kathy, my mom, my sister (Pam), and her husband (Steve) were there. Their applause and shouting came out of nowhere but was as loud as any noise I had heard on the course all day. What a rush! I had no clue of their plans to come down to the race and find a spot on the course to watch for me. It took my breath away. After a brief smile, acknowledgement, and thank you, I had to keep moving. That quick moment motivated me to finish strong. I felt like the Grinch when his heart grew three sizes. My family being at the 20-mile mark was like winning the lottery. I finished my first marathon without stopping and the surprise at the 20-mile mark was the reason I was able to accomplish it. Nothing else motivated me more that day.

If you want to do something special for a runner in your life, surprise them on the course! Don't tell them that you plan to be on the race course. Think of it as their 20 seconds of fame. Learn about the course and consider a location beyond the halfway mark. Many race spectators plan to meet at the finish line amidst hundreds or thousands of people. Be different, and find a spot on the course to surprise your runner. My family went through all that trouble to plan a 25-mile drive to the race, set up, then wait for me to run by. They saw me for 20 seconds, and then they drove home. They didn't try to compete with the foot traffic and parking near the finish line. That was a powerful motivation I never saw coming, and one I will never forget.

Note to self: Always look for opportunities to support others in unique ways.

"Ants Marching"

Perception is a funny thing.

Everyone has firsts. My first marathon in downtown Cleveland involved a running moment that I never saw coming. Training for a marathon is a challenge. The 26.2-mile event is tough by itself, but it's the practice that really wore on me. It took so much time away from my family, that I often wondered, *why am I out here running?* Each week consisted of a long training run over the weekend for 16 weeks. Regular runs, speed workouts, and a long weekly run were all par for the course. I peaked at an 18 mile run and then tapered off every week leading up to the marathon.

To prepare for my first marathon, I was given a training plan by a co-worker. I followed it religiously. I had two goals for my first marathon. One, run the entire race without stopping. And two, don't set a goal for time. I was told that time goals will mess with my head going into my first marathon. Besides, time goals will come naturally with experience. Even now, I believe these are the smartest goals for first time marathoners. Co-workers who had completed marathons gave me this advice, and I stuck to it.

It made sense to not set a time goal as I had never run a marathon distance at one time. Meaning, once I established a time at the end of my first marathon, I will have a reference upon which to improve in all future endurance races. If I hit the wall at 18 miles into my second marathon (as I did), and at 20 miles in my third marathon (as I did), it will allow me to reflect on how much I enjoyed the simple goals from my first marathon.

It was race day morning. I was with a group of four gentlemen and one lady as the runners spread out. We were moving pretty quickly (7:30/mile pace) and comfortably heading into a neighborhood. I did not know this group of runners. I never spoke to them before, during, or after the race. We were drafting each other. If unfamiliar with this concept, it's when groups of runners take turns leading the pack. Runners do this in order to share the resistance and energy required from being in front. There are many articles written on the advantages (or disadvantages) of drafting while running. I will leave the debate to the experts. But the six of us were switching the lead position to benefit the small group by drafting.

While running near the curb in this neighborhood, the young lady in our group veered off to ask a question to an elderly couple sitting in their lawn chairs. I saw them shake their heads "no," and I immediately thought, *oh please, let her use your bathroom.*

"ANTS MARCHING"

Perception is a funny thing.

The young lady rejoined our small group. She was a skilled runner, as she not only caught us, but took the lead in our small drafting group after her brief conversation with the elderly couple. I assumed whatever she had asked the couple had motivated her to run even faster which allowed her to catch back up to our group. Nobody asked her anything as we kept gliding near mile four. Up ahead was an intersection with a traffic light. I watched her veer off again and ask a police officer a question. I watched the officer shake his head "no." This time, I noticed that she was in tears at the negative response, and I thought, *I can't imagine needing a bathroom at the fourth mile of a 26.2-mile marathon.*

Perception is a funny thing.

She was devastated by the news that there was no restroom nearby. With so many thoughts that went through my mind during my marathon, I lost track of that moment and didn't think of her again that day.

I had traveled to this race with my co-workers from Indiana to Ohio. We drove home in one car each sharing stories about our exciting day. My conversations with my group of co-workers included seeing a guy dribble a basketball while jogging the event along with another guy flipping a pancake in a pan while running the course. I shared how terribly sore I was right after the race. I had to immediately sit on a curb because I could not walk another step within 30 seconds of my finish. But I never shared the story of the young lady needing to use the restroom.

The next evening, the national news shared a tease prior to the commercial break that they would have an interesting story from the Cleveland Marathon which took place yesterday. I called excitedly to Kathy that a story was forthcoming on the marathon I ran yesterday! There was no social media at the time, no Twitter or Facebook where I might find the story instantly. So Kathy and I waited patiently for the commercials to end.

Perception is a funny thing.

When the news returned from the commercial break, the anchor reported that in the Cleveland Marathon yesterday, a young lady started running in what she thought was a 10K race, but she was really in the marathon race. The female runner appeared on the screen, and it was the same young lady I was running with the day before! My jaw hit the ground. I was speechless. The young lady on the screen explained that she got worried as she was unsure if she was running on the 10K race course. She asked a local couple sitting on their lawn if this was the 10K course. They were not sure. She asked an officer at an intersection if he could take her back to the start line, as she thought she was in the wrong race, but the officer could not. Large city road races typically have multiple distance events. They either start at different times or all runners start at the same time and then are redirected on the course to their appropriate race distance (5K, 10K, etc).

She stated she saw someone run by her with a running motivational t-shirt, so she proceeded to run the marathon. She had never run further than eight miles at any one time. Her family became very worried when she did not come in with the other 10K finishers. She ran an approximate four-hour marathon, which is very respectable.

I was relieved to discover that she did not need a restroom after all. I laughed at myself for being fooled by the situation. This runner decided to run further than she had before, and yet she had no plans to conquer a marathon distance that morning. I cannot imagine making a spur of the moment decision like this with respect to a race. Planning for a marathon requires so many more training miles versus a 10K plan, for example. That's the physical part, but the mental part is also a night and day difference between a marathon and a 10K.

If I had found myself in a situation where I had registered for a 10K race, but ended up on the marathon course, I know I would have jogged back to the start line and laughed at my mistake for years. The only way I would have finished an unplanned marathon would be in a cold sweat waking up from a dream.

Note to self: Perception is a funny thing.

"Hair of the Dog"

While growing up, my family always had a dog in the house. I loved watching them run. I marveled at their fluid motion when they were in a quick sprint. I recall that our dogs were well-trained and were always on a leash or in a fenced-in yard.

As an adult running the roads across America, I have experienced my fair share of run-ins with man's best friend. I have a pet peeve about folks who don't secure their dogs on leashes or with invisible fences, but allow them to roam the neighborhood. This frustration comes from a time when I delivered newspapers as a kid. I had a customer who would see me come to collect money for the previous papers delivered, grab hold of her dog's collar while inside the house, then open the door as she held back her angry dog. I dreaded that one house every day, whether delivering the newspaper or collecting from the customer. Once, she did not have a grip on the dog's collar, and the dog lunged at me, locking onto my wrist for a couple of seconds. Thankfully, the family member who opened the door reacted promptly and pulled the dog back into the house. This memory comes back whenever I find myself in the path of a dog on one of my runs.

One such dog encounter happened to me on a run in Fort Wayne, Indiana. I was on a weekend run between three housing divisions. I decided to go out for a 5K run in the heat and humidity. I was on my return from an out-and-back course, running on the concrete street near the curb. Approximately four to five houses ahead of me, I heard a dog barking intensely at a young mother pushing a baby stroller on the sidewalk on the opposite side of the street.

"Cujo" was ripping down the driveway and about to head into the street. My immediate thoughts were, o*h please don't attack this lady and her baby. Where is your owner? Why do people leave their dogs free to roam?* Just as the dog reached the end of the driveway, a gentleman washing his car came yelling for the dog to stop. Cujo stopped just short of entering the street. The dog trotted back to his owner who took hold of Cujo by his collar. I felt relieved for this young mother and her child. My turn was next.

My mind flashed back to the many articles I have read about running and dogs. I've learned that no matter how hard I am breathing, I should not show my teeth to a dog when running. I should avoid the dog and not charge it or challenge it. Countless times I have altered my running course because of a loose dog.

"HAIR OF THE DOG"

I know many have barks worse than their bites, but it's all about risk analysis. I have also carried dog snacks in my pockets while running, just in case I needed a decoy. Still, as an animal lover, I hate to see pet owners leave their pets loose, which only causes angst among people who simply want to walk or run in their neighborhoods. I felt some comfort knowing that if Cujo decided to come after me, his owner was nearby ready to save the day during my current run.

Out of an abundance of caution, I moved over to the opposite side of the street from Cujo and hoped he wouldn't see me. Who was I fooling? I could see the dog's owner was still outside washing his car. As I ran by, I heard the first intense bark as Cujo decided I was breaking neighborhood laws by running that day. Cujo must have been recruited for the neighborhood watch program, and I was up to no good. *Can't I run on the public streets and sidewalks?* The bark was followed by the dog's nails digging into the concrete, a sound that has never left my memory. The feeling immediately raised my blood pressure, even though I somewhat expected this result.

As predicted, Cujo had his laser eyes locked on me for his midday snack. Just as the dog reached the end of the driveway, his owner hollered again at the top of his lungs for Cujo to stop. Cujo entered the street this time, but he did listen to his owner once again and stopped on a dime. I swear I heard Cujo mumble, "I'll get you," as he looked over his shoulder at me in disappointment and trotted back to his owner.

I had to seize the moment. I stopped, looked directly at Cujo's owner, and tried to say as politely as possible, "I would really appreciate if you would keep your dog on a leash." Being out of breath, and with my blood pressure spiked, I'm sure it came across as a command. I guess the old adage is true that it's not what you say, but how you say it.

Cujo's owner immediately responded with the same intensity as me and replied, "It's not my dog!"

I reduced my tone and gratefully thanked the gentlemen for saving me from Cujo. I turned quickly and ran home. For the first 30 seconds, I swear I heard nails scratching the concrete as I envisioned Cujo's "non-owner" releasing Cujo's collar, allowing him to lock in on the target on my back. It was only my imagination, and I lived to run another day.

Note to self: Don't jump to conclusions. They can bite.

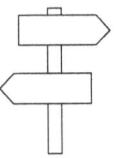

"Another Song about the Rain"

Once when my daughter, Haley was running with her cross-country team, I thought I might join them. So we gathered in a local park with the boys' and girls' teams. I was feeling good that morning, so I decided to run with the guys after discussing it with the coach, Bill Dennison. I was confident I could keep up with them. It was a nice fall morning with a little humidity in the air. I knew there was a good chance of rain, but the morning was sunny, so I decided to risk it.

I was able to keep the pace going with runners probably 30 years younger than I, mainly because we were running on flat surfaces. Running with these guys brought back memories of being younger and faster. I felt pretty proud of myself for keeping up with the group, even if it was just a training run for them. For me, it was a brisk pace, but I was comfortable, exposed to fresh air, and ready to seize the day.

After about two to three miles though, we hit a significant

hill and then started to wind through some unfamiliar roads. As I faded to the rear of the group due to the hill, I thought, *no problem.* Bill was very gracious and asked me if someone should hang back with me at my pace, but I declined. I still felt confident that I could keep the group in my sight, even though I struggled with the hill and some unfamiliar roads.

Who was I fooling? Pretty soon the group was so far ahead of me that I would lose them on turns. *But at least I can see the group turn left or right,* I thought. That shot of confidence eventually faded when I could no longer determine which way the group had turned. I was in a rural area running by field after field with very few landmarks to guide me. *Somehow my path will cross with the guys.* But the truth was I saw no other runner, walker, or breathing human for the next 15 minutes as I continued to venture deeper into unfamiliar territory. *Why are there no cars out here?*

I was lost. I knew what city I was in, but I couldn't tell you exactly where I was within the city. *A recognizable landmark must be coming up.* We had made so many turns I truly couldn't tell north from south or east from west. It became very cloudy, so the sun was hidden and not providing me any sense of direction. Then, it started to drizzle. *How appropriate. I deserve this for thinking I could run with teenage cheetahs.*

The clouds turned darker. My anxiety increased because there was no place to take shelter if a hard rain hit. It wasn't long before the light rain turned into a monsoon. Sheets and sheets of rain drove downward and sideways. Lightning and thunder complemented the situation. Waves of water flowed across the road, so that my shoe created a temporary dam with each step. I had no clue which direction to go, and now I also had five-pound running shoes on each foot. But I kept running.

After some thought, I decided to reverse my path in hopes I could find my way back. A few cars had started passing me and probably thought I was a "poor fool" for being out in this rain. Little did they know, if they had stopped to ask if I could use a ride, my first question would have been, "Where am I?" That hypothetical scenario kept my mind amused and positive, as I really wanted to see someone's reaction to my question if anyone actually stopped.

Nobody interrupted my journey. At one point, I finally paused, looked up at the torrential rain, and asked, *Why me? Why am I out here?* Somehow, I found my way back to a main street which I knew well enough to determine which direction to go to head back to the park where we all began. I was approximately three miles away, and the rain had still not let up. I continued to slosh forward with each step, and the monsoon rain calmed to a solid downpour. *Lucky me, eh?* I was a little worried as Haley would be back at the park, probably wondering where I was.

When I finally made it back to the park, the entire boys' team had returned and rested, and some had left for home with their parents. The girls' team had just finished, so the potential worries my daughter may have had never materialized.

She didn't even notice that I arrived by myself. I asked her how her run was. She replied that it was "a normal training run with a little rain." *A little rain?* Then she returned the same question to me.

I replied with a short response: "unique." When she reads this story, it will be the first time she realizes just how unique my run really was.

Note to self: When coaches give advice, take it.

1974 – With my baseball coach & gym teacher Rik Danburg.

2017 – Working together with Rik in the Mentor High School press box.

1978 – Running around during a family vacation in Deep Creek Lake, Maryland.

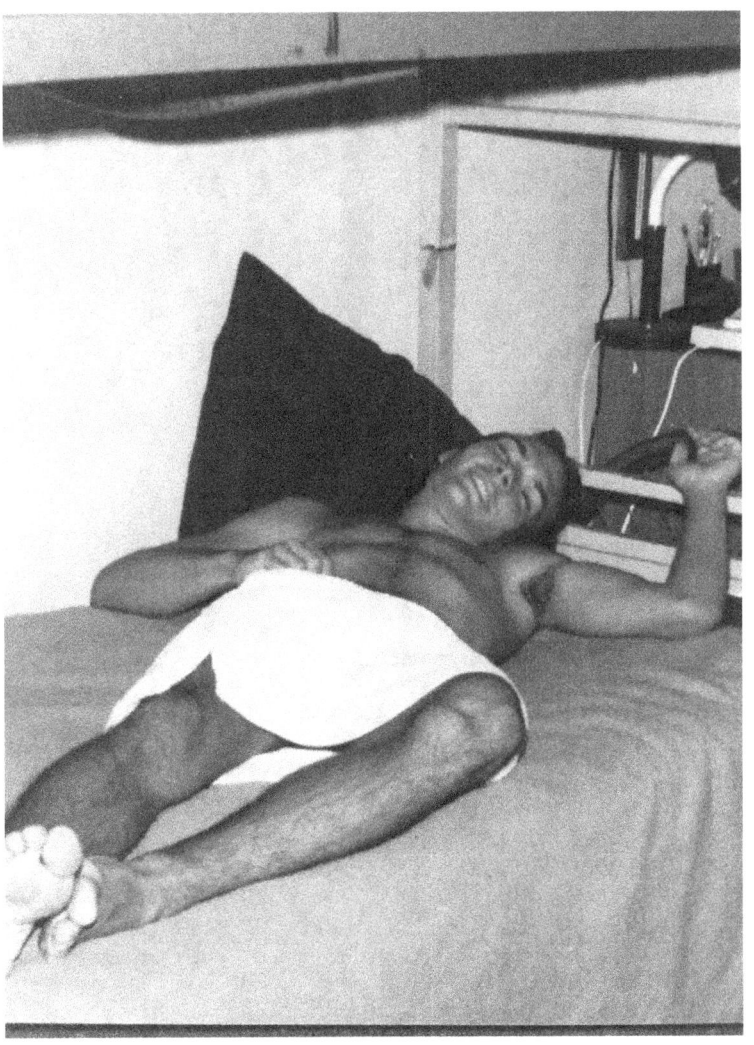

1980 – After my first road race
(4 mile race in college).

1986 – Family picture with our beloved Rascal
(Go figure ... in running clothes).

1986 – Fort Wayne, Indiana race.

1986 – Fort Wayne race with a cool shadow effect.

Late 1980's – Prediction race in Fort Wayne.

1989 – 1st marathon in Cleveland, Ohio at the 20-mile mark when my family surprised me.

1989 – 5-mile Johnnycake Jog in Painesville, Ohio.

1989 – Sore, stiff legs after the 5-mile Johnnycake Jog.

1991 – My license plate while living in Williamsburg, Virginia.

1999 – Signing up for a 5K race in Newport Beach, California.

2004 – Tiki hut & tortillas in the Bay to Breakers race in San Francisco, California.

2015 – From left, daughter Haley, me, and Haley's friend Kelsey at a downtown Cleveland Race.

2015 – My all-time favorite race shirt. Is it a baked potato or a sunset behind a mountain range?

2019 – Downtown Willoughby 5K
Photo credit: Capstone Photography

"Once Bitten, Twice Shy"

Sometimes I find myself in bizarre running situations when I least expect it. I was minding my own business on a Sunday morning run through a couple of large empty parking lots near my home in Mentor, Ohio. It was quiet and peaceful with very few cars or people nearby. I had moved from the concrete sidewalk to the parking lot since it was a blacktop surface, and blacktop is softer on the joints than concrete. As soon as I stepped off the concrete, a bearded gentleman moved out of a tall bush next to the parking lot about 10 yards in front of me. He was probably walking nearby, and I just didn't see him. It was as if I were driving on a highway, and he was about to merge into my lane heading the same direction. It really didn't startle me; I simply moved over to "change lanes" to allow him room to merge into the foot traffic, which consisted of only two people occupying an ocean of empty parking spaces.

I passed him without saying hello, as our eyes never met.

About five seconds later, I started to hear someone breathing pretty hard behind me. *Whoa!* I turned around, still in stride, to find the same guy following me in a dead sprint. *What is he doing?*

The long-bearded guy was dressed a little raggedly and did not appear to be a runner. I simply kicked it into another gear so my admirer could not keep up. But I could still hear him behind me, breathing hard, while falling back due to my pace. *Who does this? Was he someone I had previously sprinted by at a race finish? Was he waiting for his moment of redemption to outrun me in a parking lot rematch?*

I never understood his intention, nor did I care to ask. I was afraid of the answer. I continued running this same course for years, but our paths never crossed again. I could only guess he took up a different sport.

Flash forward a few years. I was in downtown Cleveland for a health walk. I signed up to participate through my employer, one of many event sponsors. It was a large event, and there were thousands on hand for the walk. We gathered inside Jacobs Field, home of the Cleveland Indians. I decided to run, rather than walk the course that morning. I figured I could say "hello" to my work colleagues, run the course, then wait for my colleagues' return from the walk to join them for the post-event festivities. I was joined by only a handful of others who ran the course that morning, and none of us ran together.

The event began and we headed north on East 9th

Street toward Lake Erie. I moved up front and got far ahead of the walkers. I ran on downtown city sidewalks past many front entrances of hotels, shops, and restaurants. It was Sunday morning, so there was nobody around except the volunteers on the course about to guide the onslaught of walkers behind me. I had just passed an entryway to a business, and I heard a little shuffle. As I glanced over, it appeared to be a man sleeping at this storefront. The next thing I knew, I heard huffing and puffing behind me. I looked over my shoulder to see a man chasing me on the sidewalk. A stranger seemed to be chasing me again!

He was not the same gentleman who joined me in the Mentor, Ohio parking lot for a jog, but I had immediate feelings of déjà-vu. Again, I shifted into gear and never looked back. I shared this story with my co-workers after the event. They found it amusing while I was still nervous, looking over my shoulder.

Note to self: Don't run at walking events.

"Shapeshifter"

I once had quite a bit of skepticism about the running shoe industry. I was running in regular tennis shoes when I started my journey, and I believed the industry was ripping off consumers with expensive running shoes. My running friends told me I really needed to invest in quality running shoes. So one day, I broke down and purchased my first pair of running shoes, the Adidas Oregon. *Oh my. What a rush!* It's still one of the largest running transformations I have experienced in my lifetime. I went from running in shoes to running on pillows. After my first pair of Oregons, I moved onto my second, and then third pair of the same shoes. Then, Adidas discontinued the model, and I moved on to another shoe company. Adidas has since brought back the Oregon over the years, but I had already switched to my next manufacturer.

I left the Adidas family for Asics shoes for probably the next 20 years. The Asics brand seemed to be growing in popularity based on all the shoes I was observing at road races. So I jumped on the Asics bandwagon. I found myself taking notice of the different running shoes. This is how I would start my investigation of investing in my next pair. I didn't even need to sign up for a race. I would attend races and talk to runners about their shoes. I received my best, and most honest, opinions from my running colleagues. Also, I made a few new friends by chatting about shoes because most runners like to talk about this subject.

I bought a few pair of Asics running flats over the years along with a couple of different models. Racing flats are a type of running shoe typically used by long distance runners. They are known for their lighter weight and lack of a substantial heel. I will never know if the racing flats helped me become faster, but I felt that they put me in a better mindset for the race. I was training in heavier shoes, so racing in a flat gave me more confidence that I could pick up the pace. I felt as if I were running barefoot and natural, yet still had minimal protection and support for my feet. I would only use the racing flats during actual race events, and I never trained in them. After a pair or two, I realized I wanted more durability, so I moved onto different Asics models. Although I stuck with the brand for approximately 20 years, and over a half dozen different models, I felt the shoes were starting to get too heavy for my running style. Their quality and durability were awesome, but I felt sluggish. It probably wasn't the shoe, but my old body feeling the effects of many years of running.

I left the Asics brand and transitioned to Mizuno, which I

"SHAPESHIFTER"

run in to this day. My local running store recommended the shift as I was looking for a lighter, yet durable, shoe. I landed in the Mizuno Wave Rider series and continue to buy the next model. I currently rotate my Mizuno Wave Rider 20, 21, and 22 models with each run. I learned over my running years that it helps to have multiple pairs of running shoes so your feet aren't subjected to the same wear and tear. I have a system with three pairs of active running shoes. I rotate them for each run and replace the oldest pair after about 500 miles. I keep a record of each run, which includes the shoe I wore. I do this to track the mileage on each pair of shoes. I selected the 500-mile milestone to replace a set of shoes because I start to notice the shoe is breaking down at that point. The shoes still feel great to me after 500 miles, but I can see that I start wearing through the first layer of rubber on the sole or that the stitches on the uppers are giving way.

Maybe three pairs is too many to run in, but I have found it to be a system that protects my joints and has kept me running for many years. For those who have their doubts about the benefits of actual running shoes, take it from me, my life changed once I invested in my first pair. I liked them so much, I needed a shoe rack.

I always donate my old running shoes. My local running store has a donation box. Other organizations may accept shoes to be reused. If I didn't have a donation box available, I would contact the shoe manufacturer to inquire how to salvage the shoes. I figure they have a good ideas on how to recycle to better save our planet.

When a revolution occurs, I believe it opens one's mind to change. A psychological shift occurred when I invested in my first pair of running shoes. It convinced me to train even harder in hopes of running longer and faster. Of course, I was still young and hadn't realized that one should run for the health of it.

Note to self: Change is good.

"My Body"

When I run, I often find myself thinking about a hundred different topics. Even when I physically sense the wind conditions, or hear the hum of cars, or smell flowers or oncoming rain in the air, my mind is always thinking about something. I feel as if I am almost in a dream state sometimes, yet in a very conscious mode. Maybe this is the runner's high many refer to. I'll leave that discussion to those far smarter than I.

Whether I run a 5K or a marathon, hundreds and thousands of thoughts go through my mind during the process. I typically jot down some of these thoughts when I finish my runs as it is fun to reminisce about them in later weeks. Written comments in journals have turned into typed inputs on the computer.

One time I was daydreaming while running in Mentor, Ohio in a brand-new subdivision. It was a lovely autumn weekend. Nobody lived in the subdivision yet, but there were many houses under construction. The phase one houses were not being built near the entrance to the subdivision, but in the rear. It was easy to see the housing trusses in the distance amid the winding roads. I had run past the subdivision entrance a few times. This time, I decided it was developed enough to run into the neighborhood and check out the new structures. The concrete road to the new sub-division was blocked off, but the surface was intact and looked as if it needed someone to perform a test run on it. It was cool to think that I would be the first person to run the streets of this new community. *Pioneer me!*

I stepped through the barriers and felt the joy of being on a brand-new street. I had to go back into the subdivision about a half-mile before I was next to the first structure. I looked left and right at each new skeletal outline and recalled how Kathy and I had watched two of our previous homes be built from the ground up. The excitement these future families will have in owning a new home was making me smile. I was far enough into the subdivision that I couldn't see the main entrance. As I was christening this new running surface and sightseeing over to my left shoulder, my right foot stepped on a rock in the center of the street. Not a small rock but one the size of a softball.

I rolled my ankle and went down quickly. Thank goodness I avoided hitting my head or any other joint against the concrete. I rolled into a crumpled state with dignity. An Olympic judge may have given me an 8.5. I immediately let out multiple screams, as I was convinced I had broken my ankle. Nobody was within earshot, so who was I kidding that someone could help me? I took very deep breaths while staring up at the sky, as I didn't want to look at my ankle. I have weak knees when it comes to injuries, mine or anyone else's. I'm sure there were a few tears amidst the sweat. How could I be so ignorant not to pay attention to the road which was still a dangerous construction zone? Still lying in the center of the street resting on my elbows, I finally looked at my ankle. It didn't look as bad as it felt which calmed my nerves a bit.

I scooted on my rear to get away from the rock to the edge of the road. I was staring at the rock while moving toward the curb. I felt the rock wanted more of me. All I was really doing was scratching my running shorts on the concrete, thinking the pain would magically go away if I moved away from the accident site. I laid near the curb for several minutes, watching my ankle begin to double in size. *How am I going to get home? What if I am stuck here for hours? Kathy will be worried to death and probably won't think to glance down this new construction road to search for me. After all, the street is blocked off. Who would venture down this street? Pioneer me!*

After 10-15 minutes, I decided to get up and try to put pressure on it. *No way.* I was stuck, unless I wanted to hop on one foot for approximately a half-mile in hopes of flagging down someone. I sat and gave it another 10-15 minutes. After that, I stood. This time, I could walk but could barely put any pressure on it. After attempting a few steps and getting nowhere fast, I did something that surprised even me.

I thought, *What would happen if I start to jog on it?*

To my amazement, I could run on my damaged right ankle. The pain was minimal while running, and nothing like the piercing pain I felt when I sat idle or tried to walk. I stopped running to challenge my odd findings, as I could not believe my body was reacting this way. How can an ankle have so much pain when idle or trying to walk, but move with little pain when running? Yep, my ankle pain was immediate if I walked or let it sit idle. So I ran home, which was probably 1.5 miles away, on a problem ankle. I still find it intriguing to this day.

I got back home with a story to tell Kathy and an ankle that needed some attention. I iced it and went for an x-ray. It was not broken, just severely sprained. My doctor told me to stay completely off the ankle for a week, not to run on it for six to eight weeks, and to use crutches. Kathy told me to stop looking at new housing construction. *Pioneer me?*

Note to self: Multitasking while running is a risky thing.

"Lose Yourself"

Given the chance to stop in Lexington, Kentucky on the way home from a trip to Georgia, I knew I was going to be able to run in a state that had so far alluded me. Kathy and I were returning from a trip to visit our son, Jake, at the University of Georgia. I thought it would be cool to stay at a hotel and run around the University of Kentucky campus.

The next morning, I headed out from the hotel for an early run to traverse the campus. I had the general direction in mind to locate the university as I navigated on South Broadway. I didn't have my phone, so the directions were in my head. I ran through some off-campus housing and finally found the college grounds. I zigzagged around different buildings, streets, and sidewalks. While cutting between multiple buildings, possibly retracing some of my previous paths, I saw a long line of people standing outside a building on this quiet Sunday morning. I jogged by the group, thinking I could figure out what they were in line for.

As I got near the end of the group, I gave up trying to figure out why so many people were present, so I decided to ask. I think they thought it was crazy that I didn't know the crowd was lined up for a Wildcat basketball practice. Maybe I should have explained that I was from out of town as their eyes shot lasers through me for not knowing the basketball practice schedule. *Go figure.*

I continued my run past the football stadium which was bustling with construction vehicles blocking off the majority of the perimeter. I ran around the entire football stadium hoping to find an opening where I could sneak inside to see the interior. No luck, so I pushed forward.

It was probably time to start heading back to the hotel so Kathy would not worry about me being gone so long. I had been out gallivanting for 45 minutes, which is longer than a normal training run, and I hadn't even started to head back yet. I navigated through campus until I was in off-campus housing that did not look familiar. *Something will come up to remind me where I was and in which direction I need to go: a street name, a unique house I saw on the way in, any landmark…any human being would be nice right about now.*

I continued to run. Nobody was around, so I just kept running with thoughts of Forrest Gump in my head. The sun's location was not clear to me as the day was completely overcast. I use the sun to help me with general directions when needed. So I just kept running, turning corners, and hoping I could find someone who could help me. Nobody was around! I really started to get worried, not for me, but for Kathy. She has a pretty good timer in her head and often comments to me, "you were away for some time on that run," or, "that didn't take you too long." She was probably wondering why I wasn't back yet for breakfast. I just wanted to find any breathing human to ask for directions to South Broadway. Simply put, I was lost.

I continued for about 20 more minutes of random zig-zagging through off-campus areas. Still, nobody. *Did the apocalypse occur? How could I be so unlucky to not come across a landmark which I recognized?* Finally, in the distance I saw a group of runners. As we approached each other, I slowed down to ask for the directions to South Broadway. The runners gave me the same look as the fans in line at the basketball practice.

Their directions included a few turns, and I finally found myself on South Broadway. Now, which direction to run? I had a 50/50 chance going either left or right. I chose left for no college educated reason. My gut guessed correctly, and I eventually recognized some landmarks guiding me back to the hotel. My one-hour-plus run had not worried Kathy, but it certainly got me all worked up, not to mention some pretty sore muscles.

Note to self: Leave breadcrumbs the next time I run in a new area.

"Machinehead"

One day at work, some of my runner friends were talking about an upcoming biathlon which consisted of a 5K run, followed by a 20-mile bike ride, then another 5K run. Because I had never raced on a bike, I had no interest in participating. But my co-worker, Phil, had a suggestion for me. Phil had a buddy, Rob, who was a cyclist, but not a runner. We could sign up as a two-person team, in which one person runs the 5K while the other person bikes the 20-miles, followed by the same runner legging out the final 5K. Phil thought Rob and I would be a great team, as I was a pretty quick runner, and according to Phil, Rob was an "animal."

I laughed out loud imagining what an animal on a bike might look like. "What do you mean by your description?" I asked.

Phil grinned, "Trust me." Phil made a great sales pitch as I had never met Rob. In fact, Rob and I would meet for the first time at the upcoming biathlon.

On race day, Phil introduced us on site. We had typical athletic conversations, sharing with each other that we're "not that fast" and "not that competitive."

"What do you think your time will be?" I asked.

Rob replied, "I don't know. How about you?"

With the same humble tone as Rob, I said, "We'll see."

Rob suggested, "Let's just enjoy the early summer evening and have fun."

Rob was taller than me and looked like a pretty solid cyclist, so I felt confident that I had a strong athlete for a teammate. The race director explained that as a team, we had matching bib numbers and one wristband, which I would wear for the run, then hand off to Rob in the transition area to wear on his 20-mile bike ride. When Rob finished, he would then hand off the same wrist band back to me to wear during the final 5K. Easy-peasy, but probably a pretty sweaty wrist band by the end. *Ugh.*

It was time to start the race. Kathy attended with me so I was able to leave my excess gear with her. I also asked her to count the finishers in the first run leading up to my finish. I wanted to know what place we were in when I finished the first 5K. The running course was a simple square course. We headed out on rural roads and ran by a few subdivisions. I felt great during the first leg of the race, as the course was flat and fast. I finished the first 5K and transitioned the wristband to Rob. I caught my breath while Kathy told me I had finished 23rd. I had run fairly hard, so I felt pretty good coming in 23rd out of approximately

200 in the race.

I had to conserve some energy during the first 5K because I had a second 5K to run after Rob's 20-mile bike ride. I needed to keep my muscles loose during Rob's ride, so I kept walking and stretching and replenishing my fluids. I could not sit idle, as I would have tightened up, just as any other runner would. Kathy continued to walk with me as we waited for Rob to return. Time seemed to drag. The race director received updates from the spotters on the course regarding the cyclists and fed that information to the athletes and attendees near the transition area.

The race director reported that the first cyclists were going to be returning in about five minutes, so the runners should start getting ready in the transition area. I followed his instruction with Kathy standing next to me, only a rope between us separating those in the transition area from those outside of it. The race director continued to provide updates on the approaching cyclists. All of the runners were standing near one another in the transition area turning their necks toward the farthest spot we could see on the road where the cyclists would be appearing. Finally, the first cyclist came in view, still about a quarter of a mile away. Many in the transition area continued to strain their necks and eyes to see if this might be their partner.

As the first racer approached, about 100 yards away from the finish, I said to Kathy, "That almost looks like Rob."

"Can't be," said Kathy.

Fifty yards from the finish, and we were still unsure, but it really looked like Rob.

It was Rob! My "animal" partner had soared past all 22 cyclists in front of him to ride first into the transition area leading the race. Not only was he leading, but there was no one else in sight behind him!

My stomach immediately churned as if I was going downhill on a rollercoaster. I rushed forward to get the wristband from Rob while dropping him a quick comment about being an animal. My stomach had never felt so sick during or after a race up to that point in my running career. I was now leading the race as I headed out for my second 5K. I had never led a race... ever! Within 20 yards, I could tell I had gone out too quick. My adrenaline had kicked in, and I would burn myself out by the first mile in the 3.1 mile run if I kept this pace. As much as I tried to calm my nerves, I felt as if I was failing to remain cool amid the applause from the people watching me head out on the final leg.

The first 100 yards of the run were the same 100 yards the cyclists were finishing on. I was just about to take a right hand turn off of the 100-yard stretch when I could see the second racer coming up the road, yet he was still a distance away from me before he would reach the transition area, now 100 yards behind me. We were in the lead by quite a distance.

I was able to calm down a bit once away from the crowd, but never felt comfortable, as I feared I would lose the lead and all the animal work Rob had accomplished. But I was able to get in the zone and take it step-by-step, paying close attention to my breathing pattern.

I stayed focused…until I heard footsteps. I was trained to never look back, so I maintained my focus and stride, only to hear the footsteps and breathing behind me get louder and louder. The person I heard breathing passed me. *I blew it, but 2nd place isn't bad… Oh no, are those more feet I hear behind me now that I have been passed?*

To my huge disappointment, three people passed me during the final mile of the 5K. When the first person passed, I was disappointed. I knew someone would catch me. Heck, Rob caught 22 people! When the second person passed, I got mad at myself for not having the same cheetah ability as the first two runners who passed me. When the third person passed, I was crushed. I recalled that the awards were going three deep in the team category, and I was now in fourth. I blew it and felt so bad for losing the lead for Rob.

I finished strong in fourth place overall. To my surprise, one of the gentlemen who passed me was an individual competitor. That meant that Rob and I had taken third place in the team competition, and I was now feeling pretty good about that accomplishment. *Whew!*

> **Note to self:** If an athletic teammate is an "animal," bring antacids to the event.

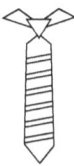

"Basket Case"

I think of myself as a curious person. As both a businessman and an avid runner, I wondered what it would be like to combine these two interests. During one point in my professional career, I was lucky enough to work at a company that supported an on-site health club. The health club had approximately 400 members, operated by the employees. My curiosity got the better of me, and I decided to get actively involved in the health club. I served in different board positions over the years, including one year as president. I remained active as a runner while promoting exercise within the workplace. I found myself sharing my running stories and exercise benefits with new and potential members.

One responsibility I had as the president was to lead the annual "State of the Health Club" meeting with our members. We were fortunate to hold this meeting away from our work site where we would serve beer and pizza to our members.

Although our company subsidized the health club 100%, we thought the employees should put some skin into the effort. So we charged $30 for the annual fee. The health club bank account increased in value every year as we had very few expenses. Once we had the approval to hold the annual offsite event, all we had to do was find a location that would tolerate us (runners like their fair share of beer).

The evening of the annual event finally arrived. After I put the audience to sleep with the latest news, financial health, and club goals, it was time for door prizes. With our cash cow bank account, we were able to provide some pretty nice awards. I can't recall the different prizes, but I remember how everyone was talking about them for weeks prior to the event. We wanted everyone to eat, drink beer, socialize, and maybe hear about the health of the club, but we all knew everyone really wanted to win the free gifts. *Nobody wants to hear about how membership has grown in the past year?* A few people asked what time we would we be drawing the prizes so I knew the crowd was anxious to move forward.

At last, it was time for the giveaways. Winners had to be present to collect their prizes. When I called the first winner's name, everyone looked around for him. Typical comments started buzzing through the crowd. "We just saw him." Or, "I know he's here." The winner's friends got up to start looking for him. We wanted to present the prizes one-by-one so we could greet each winner, rather than move on. Finally, we heard he was heading in from outside...where he had been smoking. *The irony!* A health club member was outside smoking. Even I couldn't hold a straight face. The audience had a good laugh about that, and all I could do was hope our company management sponsors were not in attendance. I think it took ten minutes from the time we drew the winner's name until the crowd got over their laughter before we could move onto the second door prize.

After getting the group settled down, we drew the name for the second door prize. He was actually in the audience and not outside smoking. *Outstanding!* Maybe our club could save face. Our winner stood up, walked forward to collect his prize, followed by a series of loud glass breaking around him. Those near the winner flinched at the sound of the glass busting on the hard floor. Those far away stood up to see what the noise was. Our second door prize winner had stood up and proceeded to drop the little glass liquor bottles he had stashed in his pockets. I guess beer wasn't going to be potent enough, so he brought his own booze. The unbroken bottles were still rolling away on the floor as he made his way forward. Some folks in the crowd grabbed them, as others scurried away from the shattered glass. *Chaos.*

We now had a large clean-up project on our hands. Because we had rented the facility for the event, a few folks started searching for cleaning products. We found a broom, a mop, a pail, and rags in a closet, so a few of us cleaned up the remains of the liquor train wreck. The crowd was hysterical. Once again,

I had lost the audience. After the clean-up and crowd control, we presented the prize to the winner. It took us about 25 minutes to present two door prizes. Thankfully, everything proceeded as normal after that. *What a relief!* Nobody will recall what I said during my presentation. However, the audience will never forget the disaster of giving away free merchandise.

Back at work, we comically reminisced about the event in meetings, at the coffee machine, and in the hallways for weeks. So much for my curiosity of combining business with running.

Note to self: Even athletes have their vices.

"Float On"

Race sponsors typically provide participants a t-shirt for entering road races, and even give away medals for winning finishers. People run races for different reasons, and each of those reasons is personal. I like to attend races where they give away random door prizes. I enjoy that all participants are eligible for these awards and not just the fastest in the field.

At one race, I won the grand door prize! It was a two-day, complete health evaluation from a local hospital. The hospital had opened a new department called the Human Performance Center where individuals could learn about their own health. Some may think *oh no*, but not me! I was thrilled to have had my name drawn to take part in this assessment. I recall them announcing that it was a $600 prize.

I was excited to receive a general health screening evaluation, learn more about nutrition, stress management, exercise, lifestyle habits, and leave with a health risk appraisal. As part of the physical testing, I was going to have a cardiopulmonary stress test on the treadmill, a blood lipid profile to measure cholesterol, a body fat measurement, a lung function test, and a musculoskeletal assessment to test strength and flexibility. I was very eager to participate and learn more from the statistics about what was going on within my body. The effort involved a two-day visit. I was stoked.

Day one started with completing many questionnaires about my current lifestyle habits. The questions were many of the same I hear when I visit a doctor. But these questions went on forever. I figured someone came up with an algorithm to crunch all this data. I was truly looking forward to the end result: the final report about Patrick Leber. I had blood drawn on the first day, and I had to bend and twist my body to collect some data. These flexibility tests went on for over an hour.

Day two was more involved, as I performed additional physical tests. The treadmill test was cool, as they hooked me up to a breathing machine along with EKG connections. I looked like a human guinea pig on the treadmill. The local newspaper was there and put my picture in the paper for an upcoming article about the new facility.

After cleaning up from the treadmill workout, I sat in a conference room awaiting the printed results from the past two days. *I can't wait! Am I eating correctly? Is my heart rate normal for my age? Do my height and weight correlate? How flexible is my body?* They shared the results in writing, and my statistical mind was in heaven reviewing it all. After all the bending, poking, and prodding, their typed assessment indicated that I was doing everything as well as I could be doing. *What about something I can improve upon?* There were a few small nutrition instructions, but no physical fitness improvement suggestions were made. This was a little disappointing, as I was hoping they could provide some insightful recommendations I could make in my active lifestyle.

After sharing that I thought I'd hear more feedback about something I could improve in my physical fitness or personal lifestyle assessment, the assessor looked over the paperwork and said, "I see from your initial questionnaire that you I responded 'always' to wearing your seat belt when in a car."

"Yes," I responded.

"Well then, tell your friends to do the same," my assessor said.

Note to friends: Wear your seat belt at all times.

"No Time"

Riddle me this. I have won two races in my running career, but I was never the lead runner in either race.

Nobody was eliminated from the race, giving me the victories. Can you guess how I did it before reading any further?

They were very unusual races from the many I had run. This type of race has very little to do with how fast I could run. Still unsure?

It had everything to do with predicting my time! The rules were simple. Prior to the race, runners checked in with the race officials and predicted their time for the 5K. Runners could not wear watches or have spotters (non-runners on the course) sharing times with them during the run. Then at the halfway mark, a race official shared the time with all runners as they passed by. Therefore, I could hear the time for other runners nearby, but I did not know what time they predicted to finish. This was simply a hint to the runners about their pace at the halfway point. It was amusing to see contestants immediately slow down or speed up at this halfway mark based on the time they heard from the race official.

There was no time clock at the finish, just a race official calling out the time and another race worker jotting that time down while recording your name. Everything was done on paper, as these races were not that large. I would guess there were approximately 100 participants.

Runners are like machines. Because I run so much, I really learn a lot about how my body functions. I have a pretty good feel for how hills affect me, whether chugging uphill or soaring downhill. When warming up, I can tell how the sun, temperature, and humidity will impact me that day. Many times, I have gone to a road race all pumped up and ready to go hard, only to change my strategy based on the weather. The rest I get the night before influences how I should be able to run. The pre-race meals the day before and the morning of a race affect my performance. All of these elements inform me about my body whether I am gearing up for a race or simply preparing for any run.

This particular event was held in a public park in Fort Wayne, Indiana. The course was a simple loop of 1.55 miles, and we had to run the circuit twice to reach the 5K distance. It was a rather lackluster course with trees on my outside left shoulder and an open field on my right. The surface started off on blacktop, transitioned to gravel, then back to blacktop. Once the gravel road surface started, we would run up a short hill for approximately

100 yards. Although not a sexy course, it mixed two surfaces and a short hill before descending the rest of the loop back to the starting line. I liked the blend of surfaces that combined road racing features with a cross-country type feel.

Before my first race on this course, I wanted to know details about the race surface, like where to find the turns, straightaways, inclines, and declines. Therefore, I ran a few practice runs on the course in the weeks prior to the race. I'm sure others did the same to better understand the course.

The springtime weather was nearly identical both years I participated in this event. I recall it being cloudy with little direct sun, but pretty humid. My typical breakfast consisted of Cheerios, coffee, and orange juice. I might sneak in a donut on occasion.

For these two 5Ks, I was lucky enough to be very accurate at predicting my finishing time. I was less than five seconds off my predicted time two years in a row on the same course. I share this story to stress how I believe running converted my body into a calculable, well-oiled machine. It's not the fastest body, or one that can endure the longest distance, but it's a body that found a passion for running and became fairly predictable.

These two prediction races occurred in the late 1980s. Now, I run for the health of it. It took me many years to learn this insight after challenging myself with competitive racing. Don't misunderstand me, I still like to participate in races, but I might sign up for only one or two races per year now. In my earlier days, I ran 10-15 races per year. Running is simply part of my lifestyle. In 2018, I ran 154 days during the year. So, I'm running nearly every other day and still allowing myself some rest. I love the health benefits running provides. When I attend my annual physical, my doctor tells me to keep doing what I'm doing. Easy for him to say as my bones are screaming at me, "not again!"

Note to self: I'm not the fastest, but I'm fairly predictable.

"Hurt"

One of the few running-related injuries I have encountered involved doubting the doctor's diagnosis. One morning before work, I woke up with a sore right shoulder. Kathy and I speculated but couldn't agree on the probable cause. I thought it might be from the pushups I had been doing every morning for years or from sleeping on my right shoulder overnight. Kathy thought it was from me replacing, and lifting, a toilet over the weekend. Yes, a "honey-do" may have done me in. The shoulder was slightly achy during my breakfast, but nothing that would interrupt my day.

I went to work, and while going about a typical day at the office, I noticed it was getting more painful as the day wore on. By noon, I could not lift my elbow higher than 90 degrees away from my body. When I did get it that high, the pain took my breath away. It would cause me to double over while grabbing my right shoulder. This scared me, as I couldn't recall a change to my body ever coming on so suddenly. I called Kathy from work and headed to the local clinic. After a quick x-ray, which did not reveal any damage, they gave me some pain medicine, put my arm in a sling, and told me to visit an orthopedic specialist. I found a doctor right away and visited him the next day. He prescribed an MRI and said we would review it when the results were complete. I had to keep my right arm in a sling for a few days awaiting the results.

I was actually looking forward to the MRI, as I was working for a diagnostic imaging company. *I finally get to have a scan. Bring it on!*

The MRI appointment was a few days after I first experienced my pain. It also was an interesting event. I had to lie down on the patient table. Simple enough. I lay there with my right palm facing down against the table. The technician made sure I was comfortable, then asked me to rotate my right arm so that my palm was facing up toward the ceiling. Again, it should be simple enough…NOT!

What sounded so easy for me to do was just the opposite. *Oh my!* The simple arm rotation maneuvering my palm from facing down to facing up was impossible. I literally could not do it. The pain was excruciating when I even tried. It was the same pain I had experienced when I tried to lift my shoulder above 90 degrees a few days prior.

Somehow, I was able to slowly, with deep breaths, turn my palm up. I started to sweat thinking, *how am I going to hold this position?* The technician mentioned that to help me hold the position, she was going to add weighted bags to keep my arm in place. *Lovely.* As she slowly and gently proceeded to do this, my body felt even more stress. *How am I going to survive 40 minutes of this?* Once secured into position with enough weighted sandbags to build a levee, I took deep breaths and counted down the minutes until the scan was completed.

I felt as if I were being tortured. *I was looking forward to this?* Whatever fears friends expressed about being inside the gantry of an MRI scanner were nothing compared to the throbbing and constant pain running through my body like electricity. My whole body had to remain perfectly still. But, my right side was in so much pain, I desperately wanted to fidget around. I was also sweating and not feeling very well. Actually, I was sweating so much that when I finally did sit up, my clothing was soaking wet, shoulder to heel.

After the scan, the technician said, "That really shook you up, didn't it?"

Ummm…yeah!

The technician suggested I rest while sitting up on the table. Once I regained my composure, the technician helped me off the table. As she led me out of the room, my body immediately veered left, and my left shoulder slammed into the door jamb! The technician whipped around to catch me as I was about to go down. She caught me before I hit the floor, and sat me in a chair for another rest. I have never experienced my body reacting beyond my control while I was fully conscious. I really think my body was in shock, and two minutes sitting up on the table was not enough time to recover from the 40-minute torture.

When I visited the orthopedic doctor two days later, he shared the MRI results and gave me the diagnosis. I had a frozen shoulder. He then prescribed a cortisone shot. Talk about a miracle cure! I've heard from many that this didn't work for them, so I felt truly lucky that it worked for me on my first try. I also had to attend physical therapy. *Bring it on...I think.*

I asked the orthopedic doctor how this happened to my shoulder? He said based on the scan and my conversations with him, chances were very good that all of the swinging movement of my arms during my many years of running ultimately led to the frozen shoulder.

Huh? Are you kidding me?

Who has a running-related injury based on a recurring movement in their shoulder? Running is all about legs and feet. How could it have hurt my shoulder? Tell me I have a neck, back, hip, knee, or ankle problem from 30 years of running (at that time), but don't tell me it's from swinging my arms back and forth over thousands of miles. I wish someone had a camera on me when the orthopedic doctor shared that my shoulder injury had developed primarily from running. I actually told the doctor that I didn't believe the leading cause of my problem was due to swinging my arms while running. I'm not sure which look on whose face displayed the most surprise. Priceless.

Note to self: Wear and tear is real.

"Ocean Breathes Salty"

Of my hundreds, or perhaps thousands, of runs over nearly 40 years, I do have an all-time favorite. Many jaunts are tied for second, but one still leads the pack. In one day, I accomplished runs in two states bringing me closer to my goal of running in all 50 states.

There probably was a good reason why I had the mental energy to accomplish my favorite running day of all-time. While on business travel in Providence, Rhode Island, I received a call from Kathy: she was pregnant with our first child! The call came while I was having lunch with a supplier. Either during the call or immediately after the exciting news, the restaurant audio system played "All I Need is a Miracle" [25] by Mike + The Mechanics. It took us years to get to this point, so the excitement was overwhelming. It gives me goose bumps to this day.

I remained excited about Kathy's news throughout the entire trip, which ended with a run on the day I was to fly out of

Providence. I was also excited to have the opportunity to run in our smallest state. Like most business trips, it was not obvious how I was going to fit in a run. I was busy with the supplier the same evening as our lunch, so there was a serious time restriction for exercise. The only way this was going to work was to run very early in the morning on the day I was to fly out of Providence. How early? 4:00 a.m. early! I dragged myself out of a deep sleep and forced myself to venture out onto a very dark highway still pumped about the news the day before.

That morning, I saw very few cars and even fewer street lights as I ran. *Am I crazy to be risking myself out here just to highlight the state of Rhode Island?* I decided to run out and back on a nearby highway for an approximate 5K while freezing my butt off.

What made this my all-time favorite run? I've only shared half the story. After my run, I had a 7:00 a.m. flight out of Providence heading to Portland, Oregon. My plan was to fly all day with a layover, have dinner when I arrived (3:00 p.m. Pacific Time / 6:00 p.m. Growling Stomach Time), then wake up the next morning and run in the state of Oregon. While in flight, I had an epiphany. What if I arrive at the hotel today and go out for another 5K? To heck with hunger! I could run two 5Ks in one day on both coasts of the United States! I arrived in Portland and could tell that my hand-eye coordination had a glitch. I was pretty tired from my family news, the early start, and the cross-country flight.

"OCEAN BREATHES SALTY"

After arriving at the Portland airport, I took the rental car to the hotel. I recall it being a gray, crisp afternoon, yet I was looking forward to venturing out. I did it. I ran along a path on the Willamette River in Portland for another 5K that day, then enjoyed a great meal, relishing my accomplishment. My face actually hurt that evening from smiling for hours. It still makes me smile every time I think about it.

Had I thought of it earlier, I would have found a spot where I could have put my feet in the Atlantic Ocean at 4:00 a.m. and then in the Pacific Ocean 14 hours later.

> **Note to self:** Life is short. Seize every unique opportunity to get in a run.

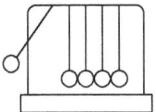

"Lucky"

As I have grown older, I have learned something important. I make my own luck. How many times are we asked to do something, but we really don't want to do it? We grudgingly decide to accept an opportunity, and some insightful moment occurs that would not have materialized had we passed on it. I cherish when these events occur, and they stick in my mind forever. One such event happened at work when a co-worker joked with me, "Why run when you can drive...and smoke at the same time?"

I have kept this question in my head for many, many years. I was asked this back in late 1980s. What a hilarious and somehow insightful question! The question contains two elements worth exploring: Why run (at all)? And if I do run, why do it when I can drive and smoke at the same time?

Why do I run? I love this question because it is open-ended and does not have an incorrect answer. There are many reasons people run. They run to lose weight, to compete, to fundraise, to build muscle strength, to reduce stress, to make them feel better about themselves, to socialize, or just because they can.

The reasons I run have evolved over the years. I previously ran because I was lucky to be pretty fast. I was competitive in my 20s and typically finished in the top 10% of all finishers. But as time (eh, age) crept up, I minimized my number of road races and realized I was running for the health of it. I started road running at 18 years old, and I kept at it. Running became a way of life, but never an obsession.

If I need to take three days off, I take three days off. If I need to rest for seven days, no biggie. If I have an injury and should take a three-week break, I take a three-week break. In 2019, I took my running gear to Costa Rica on a trip with my daughter, Haley, and her students. My gear stayed packed in my bag, and I did not run for 12 days. I was having too much fun with the group. I had surgery once that prevented me from running for three months. Done! I wanted to heal and come back strong. I believe in resting. When I was training competitively, I ran no more than five days a week. But for the past 20 years, I have been an every-other-day runner when healthy. I truly believe in the every-other-day approach. Our bodies need that rest. I believe this strategy has allowed me to continue to run for many years and experience many adventures along the way.

The second part of the question probes why do I run when I can drive and smoke at the same time. Driving has it merits.

I can see the United States and all its beauty. It allows me to get from point A to point B efficiently. It allows me to see my family and friends who are only a short distance away. But the confines of a car don't give me the rush that a run does. A convertible, bicycle, ATV, or a Big Wheel (I loved this as a kid) probably provides the closest feeling to a running rush since one can ride in the open air. So for me, I believe it's the feeling of being outside and not confined to a car. I prefer to run for the health benefit that driving can't provide.

Why does one run when one can drive…and smoke at the same time? Why does one run when one can drive…and stay warm? …or talk to others in the car? …or protect oneself from the elements? My co-worker could have mentioned any of the above actions while driving, but he chose smoking. He chose smoking to be funny, but what he was really asking me was why do I run at all? I do it for the health of it and for seeing, hearing, and experiencing things in our world I would not see, hear, or experience from inside a car. I am lucky to be able to run, and I cherish it every time I lace up my shoes.

I'm not quite sure what, why, or how I was granted the gift of glide. I am so blessed to have been physically able to run so many miles after nearly 40 years. I have a simple goal going forward, and that is to keep moving. Some will read that and say, "Yeah, whatever. We all keep moving." But, running helps me to establish a mindset that prompts me to do that. I don't park my car near the stores or venues I visit…to keep moving. I drop my passengers off, so I can park and walk...to keep moving. When I pull into my driveway, I pull into the garage before walking back to the mailbox to get the mail...to keep moving. I have a goal to never have a handicap placard for my car unless absolutely needed for myself or a guest in my car...to keep moving. I leave the TV remote further than an arm's length away to get up to change the channel...to keep moving. While doing yard work, I walk back and forth many times over the lawn to gather tools... to keep moving. When time is not critical when walking to my destination, I walk a different path...to keep moving.

My consistent efforts to keep moving have been paramount in being "lucky enough" to have run for many years.

Note to self: Keep moving ... so I can stay lucky.

"Thank U"

Thank you, Mom. You were the most devoted reader I have ever known. There was nobody who read more books than you. I know you would have wanted the first copy of this memoir to read prior to everyone else. Hopefully, people will read and enjoy these stories. I miss you tremendously.

A huge shout out to Willie & Rachel Scott (www.tkipublishing.com). Your motivation and inspiration helped push me to stop thinking and start doing. You're rock stars in my eyes.

Thank you, Andria Flores (www.andriaflores.com), for helping me through the writing and editing process. I am forever grateful you accepted the challenge to help this average writer tell average stories in extraordinary ways.

I want to thank Dr. Roger Leslie (www.rogerleslie.com) for providing his outstanding and thorough editing and proofreading services. You opened my eyes to many lessons learned.

Carly Mitchell, thank you for your cover work and story icons throughout the book. I have admired your artwork for years, and I am so proud to have watched you flourish in your career. I am honored you accepted the opportunity to share your artwork for this project.

Jake Leber served as the beta-reader for my memoir. I requested his honest feedback, and he delivered as I had hoped: "I have to admit, I don't like this story. It's boring." Input like that is exactly what I needed to hear, and I appreciated it so much. Thank you for making me a better writer. I love you.

Many of my family members provided hundreds of suggestions to improve the manuscript. Their insight was critical in helping me type my stories. I love all of you and truly appreciate your insights: Haley Leber, Kelli Amerine, Lynzi Gruetzemacher, Terri James, Patty Naumann, Pam Trivisonno, Ray Leber, and my brilliant wife, Kathy. Thank you for your support and desire to assist me with my clunky writing.

"THANK U"

My Aunt Kathi and Uncle Paul Kopasko now reside in a beach town on the Delaware shore. Thank you for living in this area, as this is my favorite recurring run with each visit. It's 2.7 miles to the beach, where I take off my shoes and socks to put my feet in the Atlantic Ocean, rinse off, and run another 2.7 miles back to your lovely home. I cherish this run and love you both for sharing your household with me and my family.

Thank you to Mr. Rik Danburg who gave me such a heartfelt response to a question I have had for many, many years in the "Given to Fly" story. Rik has been my teacher, coach, mentor, co-worker, and an overall a great friend to me and my family for more than 40 years.

I am also forever grateful to the public businesses that have allowed me to use their restrooms during a run. A few times each year, I need to find a public restroom in the middle of a run. Businesses with public restrooms have saved me from a code brown in more situations than I care to share.

I also truly appreciate the many drivers who have moved their cars over when driving by me. The roads were put there for drivers to get from point A to point B. I am forever grateful I have roads to run on, and I will always respect that roads exist for all drivers.

My appreciation goes to all my family and friends who have supported me and listened to me tell these stories over, and over, and over again, after nearly 40 years of hitting the pavement.

Thank you for reading about my running adventures. I am sure there are hundreds more, but these are the ones that stood out to me. I hope you enjoyed the stories, and that they brought a smile to your face, even if at my embarrassment. *Keep moving :-)*

Please write me at with any comments:
contact@whyrunwhen.com

References

[1] Pearl Jam. "Given to Fly." *Yield.* Epic Records, 1998. CD.

[2] Tom Petty and the Heartbreakers. "Runnin' Down a Dream." *Full Moon Fever.* MCA Records, 1989. CD.

[3] Scorpions. "Rock You Like a Hurricane." *Love at First Sting.* Mercury, 1984. Vinyl LP.

[4] Pearl Jam. "Unthought Known." *Backspacer.* Monkeywrench Records, 2009. CD

[5] The Beach Boys. "Good Vibrations." *Smiley Smile.* Brother Records and Capitol Records, 1967. Vinyl LP.

[6] Pink Floyd. "Comfortably Numb." *The Wall.* Harvest Records & Columbia Records, 1979. Vinyl LP.

REFERENCES

[7] McKenzie, Scott. "San Francisco (Be Sure To Wear [Some] Flowers In Your Hair)." *The Voice of Scott McKenzie*. Ode Records, 1967. Vinyl LP.

[8] Led Zeppelin. "Stairway To Heaven." *Led Zeppelin IV*. Atlantic Record Corporation, 1976. Vinyl LP.

[9] Chicago. "Feelin' Stronger Every Day." *Chicago VI*. Columbia Records, 1973. Vinyl LP.

[10] Dave Matthews Band. "Ants Marching." *Remember Two Things*. Bama Rags Records, 1993. CD.

[11] Nazareth. "Hair of the Dog." *Hair of the Dog*. Vertigo Records, 1975. Vinyl LP.

[12] Cracker. "Another Song about the Rain." *Cracker*. Virgin Records America, 1992. CD.

[13] Hunter, Ian. "Once Bitten, Twice Shy." *Ian Hunter*. Columbia Records, 1975. Vinyl LP.

[14] Marshall Poole. "Shapeshifter." *Totems*. Defendu Records, 2015. CD.

REFERENCES

[15] Young the Giant. "My Body." *Young the Giant.* Roadrunner Records, 2010. Digital Release

[16] Eminem. "Lose Yourself." *8 Mile: Music from and Inspired by the Motion Picture.* Aftermath Entertainment, Shady Records, & Interscope Records, 2002. CD and Digital Download.

[17] Bush. "Machinehead." *Sixteen Stone.* Trauma Records & Interscope Records, 1994. CD.

[18] Green Day. "Basket Case." *Dookie.* Reprise Records, 1994. CD.

[19] Modest Mouse. "Float On." *Good News for People Who Love Bad News.* Epic Records, 2004. CD.

[20] The Guess Who. "No Time." *Canned Wheat.* RCA Records, 1969. Vinyl LP.

[21] Nine Inch Nails. "Hurt." *The Downward Spiral.* Nothing Records, TVT Records, and Interscope Records, 1994. CD.

[22] Modest Mouse. "Ocean Breathes Salty." *Good News for People Who Love Bad News.* Epic Records, 2004. CD.

REFERENCES

[23] Hickman, Johnny. "Lucky." *Palmhenge.* Campstove Records, 2005. CD.

[24] Morissette, Alanis. "Thank U." *Supposed Former Infatuation Junkie.* Maverick Records, 1998. CD.

[25] Mike + The Mechanics. "All I Need Is a Miracle." *Mike + The Mechanics.* Atlantic Recording Corporation, 1986. Vinyl LP

www.ingramcontent.com/pod-product-compliance
Lightning Source LLC
Chambersburg PA
CBHW070949080526
44587CB00015B/2239